Spineless:

Memoir in Invertebrates

poems by

Melody Wilson

Finishing Line Press
Georgetown, Kentucky

Spineless:

Memoir in Invertebrates

ACKNOWLEDGMENTS

I'm grateful to these publications for making space for the following poems:

Archetype: "Ladybird, Ladybird"
Failbetter: "Language Acquisition"
The Fiddlehead: "Army Wife"
Oberon: "What I Want You to Know About Butterflies"
Quartet: "Sailor by the Wind"
Triggerfish Critical Review: "Octopus Dreaming"
Visions International: "Metamorphosis"
Windfall: "Rising Stars"

Kay Snow Writing Awards 2020 (2d Place) "Metamorphosis"

I would like to express my gratitude to the many poets who helped me think
these poems through, but particularly the women of Zalon. Thank you all.

Publisher: Leah Huete de Maines
Editor: Christen Kincaid
Cover Art: Sarah McConnell
Author Photo: Melody Wilson
Cover Design: Elizabeth Maines McCleavy

Order online: www.finishinglinepress.com
also available on amazon.com

Author inquiries and mail orders:
Finishing Line Press
PO Box 1626
Georgetown, Kentucky 40324
USA

Table of Contents

For Phillip,
who (almost) always carries spiders out the door

Night Prayer

I've never held a firefly
    but there's a galaxy
        in my hands—
all the elusive matter
    that flutters and glows.

The persistent animation
    of my heart
    the artless laugh of a child
        all there
    where I feel
        but cannot see.

It takes restraint
        not looking,
to demonstrate devotion
    with so much
        on the line
    a flamboyant trust
    like swallowing fire.

Ladybird, Ladybird

> *Your house is on fire*
> *and your children all gone*
> *—Mother Goose*

We were alone
      the first time
            the house caught fire.

I round the corner
      to flames rolling up the cabinets,
      across the ceiling—the kitchen
      a sheet of shimmering heat.
Linda whisks by,
      scattering chairs, emerges with the birdcage.

Sisters poured from every room
      in the house, the driveway a spectacle:
            hoses, neighbors, fire trucks.
                  Our parents pull in,
                      trunk full of food,
                      to a gaping roof and
                      wallpaper sloughing away
                      from the sheetrock.

Maybe this is why I hear clanging
      instead of rhyme,
            why I worry for children gone.
Fear scuttles the thrill of the bright beetle,
      its sturdy scurry across my nail,
            its tenacious cling
                  to a blade of grass,
                      the crack of its carapace,
                      the cinnamon flash of its secret wings,
                      the disappearing act—
                      fly away,

fly away home. Even now,
    my sisters gone,
        my children grown,
            peril stings the corners of my eyes.
I switch off the lights, twist the lock,
    mince over the slippery drive.
        The car startles at my key fob's beep—
            motion ripples behind the glass.

Ladybirds cover every inch of the car: the dash,
    the windshield, the wheel. They ripple,
        a coat of red, across the leather seat. I hear
            the creaking of their little knees,
            the mechanics of their shells,
            the rapid beats of their wings.

I press my hand against the seat,
    one crawls up my finger,
        then another.
With both hands, I scoop a worldful,
    step back,
        toss them into the sky—
        they flicker around me like fire.

My Problem with Crickets

A moon face dangles from the top bunk.
I know it's you from the page-boy
but squeeze between mattress and wall
just the same. You remain mute

as a pendulum. Or years later
when you chase me through the yard
crying, *I'll stuff crickets in your ears!*
Was I afraid of them or you?
I should have thrust out my hand—
felt the wiggle of their palps,
studied the subtle plaid

of their thighs. But I couldn't bear
the underworld of slick bodies with
vague edges. Spiders in corners, silverfish
skittering up walls. I bent down briefly once,
peered at a cricket on the porch, neither monster
nor machine. It rubbed a bendy leg
across its triangle head, pulsed on the concrete

a beat, then sprang to the grass in a burst
too quick to predict. My body played
a similar trick. The first hints were round
and sweet, but all the hidden parts,
the crevices and folds—betrayals. Music
grew heavy, all my bright joys turned

their backs. But you were smooth, grew lean
and brown, flowed into new spaces,
new roles. Frayed blue jeans, sunburned
shoulders wide as your smile. You made
new friends from down road, knew the words
to all the songs, then you started sliding into cars.

What if I had faced you instead of fleeing?
We could have unfolded it together,
the four wings, the spiracles, the eyes.
Maybe if I pried your fingers back
one at a time I would find the secret
in your empty hand.

First Encounter

Bored of squeezing snapdragons' cheeks,
impersonating my sister through their ruffled
lips, I sift petals in the soil, yellow, pink. A bean
wobbles toward me, domed creature marching
through chips. I press my finger
against the ground, up it crawls.
Eyelash feet, butterfly kisses,
up my finger and into my palm.
I fold my hands closed,
draw them to my face,
open: "Peek a boo!"

Its antennae wonder.
"Don't be afraid" I poke
its shiny shell. Smooth, cool
as orange peel, familiar as fingernail.
I blow into my palm. The creature rolls up,
tight as a pea. I am wonderstruck,
test it with a tap. It rolls over once,
rocks back, Still, mute. A magic trick? A disaster?

I drop it into the leaves and stand,
brush dirt from my dress, glance
toward the house. My mother is working
in the den, my sisters playing records. The sprinkler
chides: chhh chhh, chhh, ch, ch, ch, ch, ch, ch.
I tower in the flower bed, in my guilt,
step toward the sidewalk, look again
into the mulch. The bug ambles
toward the tomatoes, my tricycle's streamers
glitter in the breeze.

Sailor by the Wind

Velella Velella, a cosmopolitan free-floating hydrozoan
—Wikipedia

They wash up, an iridescent armada,
an unstrung chandelier, and glow
dichroic against silica stars.
Because you cannot count them,
cannot measure the ribbon they make
along the shore, you take one home,
place it on the living room altar,
tolerate the smell of desiccation,
bring it to me this January afternoon
as we huddle under blankets on your deck.

We haven't sat together for months.
We've hovered in driveways,
exchanged food and news. Now,
another wave is coming and I'm afraid
you will drift too far, so we brave
the weather, the masks,
feel our way back to each other.

The cadaver rests, dainty in my hand.
Annular rings like ages of trees,
the sturdy thumb of its sail, dried now
the shade of a skeletal leaf or the vacant
skin of a snake. Not the shock of color,
the bobbing sheet of cobalt swaying
in the sea, plump chitinous sails aimed
westward into wind.

It's getting dark, and I've been
weighing risk in microscopic bits.
I return the husk to you on my open palm.
It hovers on the dehydrated toes
of its tentacles, as if I could make a wish,
blow it loose, a corona of seeds,
populate your yard
with a blue swath of hope.

Mantis

Each   foot   placed   just so
          one   two   three   four
the twig   a catwalk   and you
          on tip toe   heroin chic
          your   scapular a ruse   innocuous
          as a leaf

Vogue
          Then a   shake of your   bootie
                    left   right   left   right   shimmy
                    settle   the digits of your
          devout   hands   pianissimo

Vogue
                    so seductive
          so easy   to believe

Rising Stars

"When might you have children?" I ask.
Your chopsticks freeze, then balance
delicately across your bowl.
You are having goma and green tea
to my California roll. Tears slip down your cheeks
before you decide to speak. "We won't" you say.
Dumbstruck, I teeter into dangerous territory.

When you were a girl, we visited Yachats,
crowded into last-minute rentals with partial views,
cooked in ill-equipped kitchens.
Before breakfast, we hovered over tidepools.
I ventured a finger, unsure, but you
slid your whole hand below water silent as glass, skimmed
urchins, startled anemones, and counted stars
as if fallen from the sky. I see you rock-perched in
red shorts, tank top; your braids reflect in the pool
as a string of bubbles rises to break the surface.

Those early mornings drained into days,
tides coming and going, and then years. You remain
enthralled with the texture of the world, and
I marvel and applaud. You lead
and I follow, our familiar inversion.
But today I watch your heart break as the
trees and sky become finite. You
see yourself a steward at the end of time, and I
cannot say that you are wrong.

The water is warming,
the sea stars are rising back into the sky,
and they have taken the children with them.

Last Season of the Good Dog

The old dog bayed every night
that summer, his eyes marbled moons.
Neighbors came around to complain,
but it didn't matter. It was my job

to pour Purina in the bowl, so I was first
to see the gash. I didn't tell anyone.
The next day, or the next, someone noticed,
raised a ruckus. *Daddy! The dog's got maggots!*

The house thrived on chaos, and this brought
everyone out the door: Daddy folded down
to one knee, pressed the cocker against the gravel,
teased the wound apart. I expected

the dog to burst like a pinata. I expected fur,
skin, then a hollow space where his spirit whirred
inside a newspaper shape. Instead, he lay quiet
as Daddy grumbled about rattlesnakes, coyotes,

poured hydrogen peroxide into the wound.
I feared his soul would drown, but the solution
fizzed up bright, the maggots squirmed,
and Daddy taped the cocker closed.

The old dog lived another while, poured
his sadness toward the moon. Daddy lived
a little longer. Crossed one long leg over
the other, told a story, popped another beer.

Army Wife

The first few roaches trace sluggish arcs across the side of the oven
as it clicks to temperature. Two months since the last fumigation,

three weeks till the next; everything's stored in plastic or the fridge.
I can't bear to smash them, can't look at them. Each antenna an

accusation, each glimpse slick bile in my throat; I keep the baby
off the floor. They bother me more in daylight—

at night, moving barefoot room to room, I close my eyes,
turn on the light, cringe at their delicate clatter.

Keys rattle in the door. He drops his kit, unlaces his boots,
eats all the way through the story of his day then cocks back

in his chair, pinches the creased fronts of his pants, spots
a roach on the toaster. With a can of Ronson

he flames the bug across the counter. It jerks first one way,
then the other, frantic. My hand hovers near his arm.

The roach contracts to its smallest self, its antennae
defeated on the Formica. He washes it down the sink,

starts hunting for another. That night in bed, he dissolves
in long smooth breaths. I unfold myself,

skim the shag carpet across the hall. In the bathroom,
eyes closed, I twist the lock behind me. The faucet drips

at the rate of my heart, my toes curl against the linoleum floor.
I flip the switch—give them a head start.

Metamorphosis

Seated on both sides of the two-way mirror
at the science museum,
we study our reflections. Your face mimics mine,

but sharper, newer. Mine is rounder; my eyes lower
until you adjust the knob,
and each of us melts into the other, a trick

of genetics or light. The souvenir photo might be
mistaken for either of us;
no one ever discerns that it is both.

"Immaculate conception," I say, to raised eyebrows
when someone does the math.
I vomited daily, fainted, observed as from a distance

while my body stretched itself from child to mother,
no intermission, no
languorous enjoyment of my long, lean limbs.

I don't recall deciding, just evolving, one stage to another,
migrating like a monarch from dark
to light. You fluttered first on a drive to Salinas. The subtlest

brush against my heart,
and in that instant,
I came to exist.

One Thing About Summer

Because of the boxelder bug's chemical defenses, few birds or
other animals will eat them
—Wikipedia

They cross the table like teenagers,
wander aimless under napkins, past wine
glasses, as if mumbling under their breath

excuse me, excuse me.
We look the other way if we can.
They coat the front window, a creeping

Venetian blind. No amount
of caulking keeps them out.
By the time July becomes August,

they repose between pages
of books, comprise abstract images
on the wallpaper, cling warmly

to lamp shades. I reached for salt once,
turned back to the stove, and found one
simmering placid in olive oil.

Hedonists in afternoon sun, informants
all over the house, they cluster on drapery,
adventure over the ceiling, drop at intervals

into water glasses. By fall they've grown
senile and catapult themselves,
curtain to hair, stick there as I flick

and swear. The porch is first peppered then paved
in carcasses, their carmine shadows stain
the cement. I sweep and sweep, but visitors

still crunch to the door. Come October, it begins
to rain. I'm almost relieved for the change.
I clean baseboards, vacuum the windowsills.

By May or June, I've nearly forgiven them.
Then I notice one, no—two novices
climbing awkwardly up the screen.

Red Flag

—after Judy Chicago

She divines her day from the thrum
of her web, her life's work,
abstract installation. Each silky
shudder an iota of information
as she strums and plucks
across the galaxy by feel.
Bite-sized Penelope, she rebuffs
the occasional suitor, ambivalent
to homecoming.

Maybe she does eat one,
once in a while.
Who can blame her?
They interrupt her weaving,
impersonate meals, snip at her weft.

It drowns out the music. He wants
to throw a veil over her senses,
as if some shimmy could ever be enough.
Oh, she takes what he offers—if she has time.
Spiderlings balloon into the breeze, transparent,
irrelevant to the work.

You would think he'd have known:
the tattoo on her belly,
the scarlet stain against her
succulent skin.

Octopus Dreaming

Pressed against
the mirrored wall of the
saltwater aquarium,
you are asleep,
but restless.
Your mantle sways,
the petite cups
along each of your
elegant arms pulse; the tips
of your tentacles twine
dozily among themselves,
in and out, sentient fiddleheads.

You cycle through your repertoire:
first you are brindle, then
all color evaporates and you are chalk.
Your funnel flutters, and you
erupt into ink. One tentacle unfurls, tenses,
and you blanche camouflage—just
another rock waiting in the reef.

The narrator proposes a script for your dreams:
> *you see a crab,* he says, *and leave the bottom,*
> *you subdue your prey in your sleep and*
> *impersonate rock.*

I perceive only the hard plane of glass as
you cleave to your replica in the mirror,
auditioning masks,
as if to ask,
is it this? *Is it this?*

Rereading Your Letters

The first thing a garden snail does
    as she unfurls into the world,
        is devour the shell that housed her.

Now she begins the long undulation.
    Season after season she scrapes
        across crabgrass and marigolds.

Her tender hood toughens with time, first to leather,
    then to the brittle carapace she carries
        through the world. I have done the same,

calcified my armor over years, spiraling farther and farther
    from the heart, each whorl wider, harder.
        Maybe this is what happened to you,

your earliest skin thickening to a tougher substance
    against struggle and loss until it hardened,
        an inscrutable film, sharp as glass,

likely to splinter or crack.
    Or maybe that's what I choose to believe.
        Memory is porous, tenderness easily forgotten,

but as I page through your letters, details drain
    from the story, as if they might not fit,
        and I wonder if I've been lying as history slips

through the cracks between words.
    I follow you back, fold in on myself,
        curl around the rough edges

smaller and smaller,
    until the two of us fit
        in a single shell after all.

What I Want You to Know About Butterflies

—for Liz

By November they're back in Mexico,
the trees throng with them. They corrugate
trunks like furred lungs molting silver
and sage. Clusters expand and contract,
cracks of persimmon shimmer through
the gray. The roosts rustle when February
warms and one monarch drops,
tumbles a beat, stretches the fingers
of her cadmium wings and flies. Then another.
The trees exhale their winter coats.

Imagine us there. Butterflies lighting
in our upturned palms, tangled in our hair.
Everything before us, our laughter, our loves—
all our sparkling shards billow around us.
They swirl, expand, strain at the seams,
then shatter, scatter in a geometry of time.
We burst into triangles of flight, our margins
ripple then fade.

I tell you this as we count your days,
the threads drawn fine, then finer.
They flurry over borders, travel north
and north seeking gravity or light.
Each small life folds into the next.
We watch in wonder as they rustle away.

They're Only Locusts When They Swarm

The one open diner for a hundred miles
is filled to the gills and glowing.
Customers pack the booths, line the banquettes,
queue up outside the ladies' room.
A waitress serves a table: meatloaf, potatoes,
burger and fries, then swoops a paper cup
from her pocket, pops it over a grasshopper,
slides a menu under, bustles toward the door.
I have already been to the bathroom.
Grasshoppers cling to tile walls, creep along
grout lines, slumber on the cover
of the incandescent light.

Servers hurry to the vestibule, cups pressed
against menus. Each tosses an insect into the lot,
where it dissolves into thousands
on the blacktop, still sticky under a
darkening sky. Aluminum pole lights buzz
to life; short sudden flights of the swarm
feature like theater in dusty beams.

One tumbles into a woman's purse. Another pulses
on the partition between banquette and booth.
The man there stirs sugar into coffee,
flicks one off the table, scrapes
the last bit of shortcake off his plate.

Meals travel on trays, kitchen to table;
insects trolly under cups, table to door.
Diners squeeze through crowded aisles.
order, chatter, eat. The swarm overflows
the surrounding fields; grasshoppers alight
on the asphalt, pause, spring up by turns,
take flight.

An Appreciation of Crickets

When day finally gives in,
the sun spreads itself
all the way across the Mojave,
turns inside out revealing its tender
reds and oranges. It drapes
its long arms over the foothills
and crickets begin to applaud.
Just a couple at first,
tentative, then others join
at intervals.

I kiss my mother good night,
then my father,
pad across the Linoleum floor,
through the bathroom,
into the big room
where my bed stands
across from my sister's.
Sleep seems impossible.
My eyes strain
for shape in the dark
as the crickets gather themselves
into boisterous appreciation,
reaching crescendo
right before I let go
of the thread.

I assume they continue
until just before I wake,
sky tinted pink,
two or three still clapping—
overzealous patrons
seated in the very back row.

Melody Wilson lives in Beaverton, Oregon with her husband and two dogs. Her first poems appeared in *A Passing Glimpse*, the literary magazine of Robert Frost Middle School, and by college (then the mother of three), she received an Academy of American Poets Award. She was poetry editor of *The Portland Review*, edited *The Portlander, Anthos,* and was founding editor of *Motes*, a small poetry journal that received an OILA. After college she had a long teaching career at Portland Community College, but the pandemic reignited her original plan. Since then poems have appeared in *The Fiddlehead, Verse Daily, Tar River Review, One Art, San Pedro River Review, Sugar House Review, ReDactions, Red Rock Review, Kestrel,* and many other publications. Her work has been finalist and semi-finalist in a number of contests across the country, including Nimrod's Pablo Neruda Award. She received a first in the 2021 Kay Snow award and recently a second in Iowa's State Poetry Society Award. She is learning to really look at insects and finds them fascinating and sometimes beautiful, though she prefers to let others handle them.